CIPS STUDY

PROFESSIONAL DIPLOMA IN
PROCUREMENT AND SUPPLY

REVISION NOTES

This

Strategic supply chain management

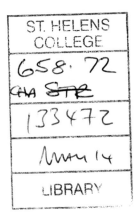
© Profex Publishing Limited, 2012

Printed and distributed by:
The Chartered Institute of Purchasing & Supply, Easton House, Easton on the Hill, Stamford,
Lincolnshire PE9 3NZ
Tel: +44 (0) 1780 756 777
Fax: +44 (0) 1780 751 610
Email: info@cips.org
Website: www.cips.org

First edition November 2012

Contents

Preface

Welcome to your Revision Notes.

Your Revision Notes are a summarised version of the material contained in your Course Book. If you find that the Revision Notes refer to material that you do not recollect clearly, you should refer back to the Course Book to refresh your memory.

There is space at the end of each chapter in your Revision Notes where you can enter your own notes for reference.

A note on style

Throughout your Study Packs you will find that we use the masculine form of personal pronouns. This convention is adopted purely for the sake of stylistic convenience – we just don't like saying 'he/she' all the time. Please don't think this reflects any kind of bias or prejudice.

Johnson, Scholes and Whittington

These notes refer frequently to a standard textbook: *Exploring Corporate Strategy*, by Johnson, Scholes and Whittington. Please note that we always abbreviate this to JSW.

November 2012

CHAPTER 1

Corporate, Business and Supply Chain Strategy

Strategic planning and levels of strategy

Strategy is 'the direction and scope of an organisation over the long term, which achieves advantage in a changing environment through its configuration of resources and competencies, with the aim of fulfilling stakeholder expectations.'

Characteristics of strategic decisions:

- They relate to the **scope of the organisation**.
- They are likely to influence the direction of the organisation in the **long term**.
- They are normally about trying to achieve **competitive advantage**.
- They attempt to match the organisation's activities to the demands of its dynamic **environment** and the potential of its **resources and competencies**.
- They will be influenced by **stakeholder** values and expectations.

JSW identify three levels at which strategic management can take place:

- **Corporate strategy** is concerned with what business or businesses the organisation is involved in or should be involved in, and the extent to which these businesses should be integrated with each other.
- **Business strategy** determines how each SBU of an organisation should attempt to achieve its objectives, in the context of the overall corporate strategy.
- **Functional strategy** determines how individual functions, such as purchasing, can best support the corporate and business strategies.

Strategic themes for supply chain management:

- The need to respond to changing environmental conditions
- Movement towards a proactive role which emphasises the strategic importance of sourcing and supply performance
- Strategies for supplier relationships
- Sourcing strategies, designed to achieve control of performance with regard to basic requirements of quality, delivery, cost and service
- Organisation of the supply function
- Application of information and communications technology (ICT)

It is important for supply chain strategies to align with business and corporate strategies: firstly, to support and enable their achievement (by securing the right resources at the right place at the right time at the right price); and secondly, to justify and reinforce SCM's strategic role and contribution.

It is in identifying objectives and identifying strategic options that the link is clearest between functional and corporate strategy. Supply chain objectives and proposed strategies must be *compatible* with the corporate strategy: various formal and informal processes may be used to bring the two into step.

Optimising the sourcing decisions: in-house or outsource; supplier selection; procurement structure; sourcing-related metrics.

Supply chain management

Reasons for increasingly strategic role of procurement:

- Change in cost base of manufacturing companies
- World class manufacturing approaches
- Emphasis on quality management
- Focus on core competencies
- Need for proactive risk management

SCM consists primarily of building **co-operative relationships** across the supply chain, so that the whole chain works together to add value for the end customer in a profitable, risk-managed and competitive way.

Effective **business processes** are another key focus of SCM.

The third main feature of SCM is **integration**: co-ordination across functional lines and organisational boundaries.

Goals and contribution of strategic SCM:

- Reducing non-value-adding (waste) activities throughout the supply chain
- Reducing total costs throughout the supply chain
- Reducing cycle times
- Improving responsiveness to customer requirements
- Giving access to complementary resources and capabilities
- Enhancing quality and service
- Improving supply chain communication
- Optimising the balance of service levels and costs
- Greater transparency for cost and risk management
- Greater supply chain visibility

Potential drawbacks of SCM:

- It requires both internal support and supplier willingness.

- There must be sufficient resources and appropriate systems in place to develop suppliers effectively.
- Investment in integrated systems, supplier development and so on may not be worth the potential gains for a given organisation.
- Increased collaboration and integration may expose the firm to risks.
- Network information-sharing may expose the firm to loss of control over commercial informational, intellectual assets and distinctive competencies.
- It is difficult to measure the effectiveness of SCM co-operation.
- There may be problems in fairly distributing the gains and risks of co-operation among supply chain partners.

SCM and business/corporate performance

Secondary objectives in support of the primary goal of profitability and survival:

- Market share
- Market position or standing
- Brand value and positioning
- Product development
- Technology and innovation
- Human resource management
- Corporate social responsibility and ethics

Supply chain management can contribute measurably to corporate, business unit and supply chain profitability in the following ways.

- **Realising revenue benefits**: either by raising the number of units sold *or* by increasing average revenue per unit sold
- **Reducing operating costs**

In nearly all cases, a private sector firm will be one of several, or many, firms offering goods or services of a particular type. Securing competitive advantage, in order to win *more* customers and *better quality* customers (higher lifetime value), is therefore a key focus of private sector strategy, including supply chain management.

The financial aspects of value creation are principally concerned with creating value for shareholders. The main aim of profitability is to generate a return on the value of shareholders' investment of capital in the business, in the form of:

- Dividends, through which a share of profits is distributed directly to shareholders
- Growth in the capital or equity value of shareholders' investment

Key sustainability issues that may be addressed in the supply chain:

- The development of reverse logistics capability
- The monitoring and improvement of employment terms and conditions for suppliers' workers
- The monitoring and improvement of standards for waste, emissions, pollution,

environmental impacts (eg deforestation) and so on
- The potential to source materials that are more environmentally friendly
- The opening up of opportunities for small and diverse suppliers as subcontractors

Commercial or business benefits of a given supply chain strategy:

- Fulfilment of a specific **business objective**
- Increased **revenues**
- Reduced **costs**
- Enhanced **profitability**
- Enhanced **value for money**
- Enhanced **shareholder value**
- **Competitive advantage**
- **Leverage** of key resources
- Increased **capacity, capability or flexibility**
- Improved **brand or reputational equity**

Supply chains and risk

Some examples of risk classifications

RISK	COMMENTS
Supply risk	Arising from supplier failure, supply failure, the length and complexity of supply chains and so on.
Compliance risk	Exposure of non-compliant or illegal activity by the organisation or its supply chains, incurring reputational, operational and financial penalties
Reputational risk	Exposure of unethical, socially irresponsible or environment-damaging activity by the organisation or its supply chain
Economic or financial risk	Risk of economic loss, as a result of poor investment or financial management, loss of sales or cost blow-outs or macro-economic factors
Market risk	Economic or supply risk arising from factors or changes in the external supply market, such as rising commodity prices, resource scarcity, the pace of technological change, or high or growing supplier power
Demand risk	Risks of fluctuations in demand for the finished product
Environmental risk	Risks of disruption or delay to supply, or rising supply costs, arising from factors or changes in the external environment of STEEPLE factors
Operational risk	Risks of operational failure, quality defects, health and safety incidents, transport failures or equipment breakdowns
Technological risk	Risks of operational problems, and resulting economic losses, due to technology obsolescence, systems or equipment failure, data corruption or theft, new technology 'teething troubles', systems incompatibility and so on.

Strategic supply risk is generally related to factors such as the following.

- Supply market complexity
- Supply chain complexity and dynamism, and the quality of supply chain co-ordination and relationships
- Vulnerability to supply disruption
- Vulnerability to fluctuations in supply, demand and price
- The financial stability and sustainability of the supply chain
- The availability of suppliers in the market
- The robustness of risk identification, assessment and management procedures throughout the supply chain.

Strategic alignment

Strategic coherence depends on goal congruence, and the 'fit' or 'alignment' of strategies in two directions.

- **Vertical alignment** is about ensuring that goals set at every *level* contribute towards the overall or higher objectives of the business.
- **Horizontal alignment** is about ensuring that the plans of every *unit or activity* in an organisation (or supply chain) are co-ordinated with those of others.

Elements in the McKinsey 7S framework

- **Strategy** is a chosen course of action leading to the allocation of the firm's resources over time in order to reach defined goals.
- **Structure** refers to the formal organisation structure.
- **Systems** refer to procedures, tools and processes that standardise work and information flow in the organisation.
- **Staff** are the human resources of the organisation: their abilities and motivation, team dynamics, flexibility, relationships and so on.
- **Style** refers to corporate image (and reputation), organisation culture (shared values, beliefs and 'ways of doing things') and leadership style.
- **Skills** refer to the distinctive capabilities of key personnel and of the organisation as a whole.
- **Shared values** are the underlying guiding beliefs and assumptions that shape the way the organisation sees itself and its purpose.

Integrating supply chain and corporate strategy:

- A formal long-term procurement and supply chain plan may be developed as part of the corporate planning process.
- Procurement and supply chain managers may be involved in the corporate planning process.
- The main board of directors may act as an integrating mechanism.
- Interpersonal relations between supply chain managers and a supportive chief executive may informally facilitate integration.

OWN NOTES

CHAPTER 2

Competitive Advantage Through the Supply Chain

Competitive advantage

Ohmae's strategic triangle, or Three Cs:

- Corporation-based strategy
- Customer-based strategy
- Competitor-based strategy

According to Porter:

- An organisation creates value – by performing its activities more effectively or efficiently than its competitors *and*
- Customers purchase value – by comparing an organisation's products and services with those of its competitors.

Porter's generic strategies:

- **Cost leadership:** seeking to become the lowest cost producer in the industry as a whole
- **Differentiation:** seeking to exploit a product or service perceived as 'different' or 'unique' in the industry as a whole
- **Focus:** targeting activities to a selected segment of the market, *either* by providing goods or services at a lower cost to that segment *or* by providing a differentiated product or service for the needs of that segment.

Five-step approach in management of cost reduction activities:

- Understand the drivers for reducing cost.
- Understand why excess costs exist in the supply chain.
- Focus and prioritise cost-down initiatives.
- Develop appropriate strategies and tactics.
- Review and measure performance.

Strategic approaches to cost reduction: restructuring; process engineering; developing collaborative relationships; applying ICT and automation; rationalising the supplier base; developing lean supply; investigating global sourcing; outsourcing non-core activities.

Contribution of strategic SCM to management of costs: collaboration on cost reduction programmes; increasing visibility of supply chain processes; optimising end-to-end supply chain costs; supporting information sharing; encouraging systems integration; creating long-term strategic relationships; supporting whole-life contracts.

Other strategic contributions of SCM:

- Creating differential advantage
- Creating time-to-market advantage
- Supporting innovation

Developing competitive competencies

Competencies are 'the activities or processes through which the organisation deploys its resources effectively' (JSW).

- **Threshold** competencies are the basic capabilities necessary to support a particular strategy or to enable the organisation to compete in a given market.
- **Core** competencies are distinctive value-creating skills, capabilities and resources which add value in the eyes of the customer; are scarce and difficult for competitors to imitate; and are flexible for future needs.

'Senior managers must conceive of their companies as a portfolio of core competencies, rather than just a portfolio of businesses and products' – and the same could be argued of supply chains.

Accenture supply chain strategy framework

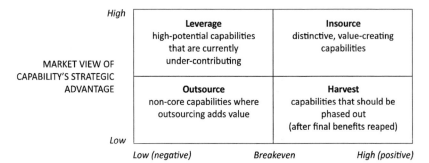

Andrew Cox's relational competence model suggests that the greater a buyer's reliance on suppliers to secure strategic competencies, the greater the depth of the supply relationship will need to be.

Ramsay suggests a number of specific ways in which an organisation can use its supply chain to develop non-replicable competencies.

- Identify and develop unknown suppliers.

- 'Enclose' a supplier.
- Apply procurement strategies which are hard for competitors to imitate.

The evolution of supply chain management has tended to emphasise the need for increasing collaboration, co-ordination and integration *within* the supply chain, in order to enable the *supply chain* to pursue competitive advantage over competitors' *supply chains* (rather than viewing competition as occurring between individual organisations at the same 'level' in the supply chain).

Enterprise profit optimisation

The discipline of EPO was developed in response to the difficulties of balancing supply with peaks and troughs in demand. Unexpected demand swings have traditionally been addressed by focusing supply management attention on two levers: levels of inventory and productive capacity. However, these are relatively inflexible: they cannot always be ramped up, or down, swiftly or economically – particularly in a global economy with long lead times for international supply.

EPO seeks to resolve this problem by converging, and simultaneously optimising, the supply and demand side of a business, using the techniques of pricing and revenue optimisation (PRO) and supply chain management.

Introducing a PRO system involves four basic steps (Cudahy).

- Segmenting the market
- Forecasting customer demand
- Optimising prices
- Dynamically re-calibrating prices

Cudahy suggests that an EPO system can improve supply chain efficiency through a four-step cycle.

- Optimising prices
- Stimulating desired demand, using differential pricing strategies
- Optimising fulfilment
- Re-optimising prices

EPO supports supply chain efficiency, profitability and customer satisfaction as follows.

- Maximising revenue returns from existing inventory (including excess inventory)
- Improving supply chain efficiency by using pricing to smooth demand
- Stimulating demand to maximise throughput and stock turn
- Enhancing profit across channels and segments
- Managing product lifecycles effectively
- Responding rapidly to changes in demand
- Responding competitively to competitor initiatives
- Reflecting strategic objectives for profitability, market share and brand image

Outsourcing

Make-or-buy decisions face all organisations, at three levels of planning: strategic; tactical; operational.

Make/do or buy decisions depend on a range of strategic and operational factors.

- Whether the item or activity is strategically important or 'core' to the business
- Economic factors: the effects on total costs of production etc
- The availability of in-house competencies and production capacity
- The availability of suitable external suppliers and positive supplier relationships
- The assessed risks of devolving activities to the external supply chain

Outsourcing is the ultimate expression of a buyer's attitude to the supply chain as an extension of in-house resources, as seen in the concept of supply chain management.

- The term **business process outsourcing** (BPO) is given to 'the transfer of responsibility to a third party of activities which used to be performed internally'.
- The term **facilities management** is given to outsourcing solutions in which the customer transfers to an external services provider the responsibility for the operation and maintenance of one or more facilities.
- The term **shared services** is given to the outsourcing of a business function to an expert *internal* department or unit.
- The term **managed services** is given to the outsourcing of responsibility for managing service operations and project activity.
- The term **in-sourcing** is given to the reverse process: the transfer of an outsourced function to an internal department of the company, to be managed by employees.

Robert M Monczka argues that outsourcing is best regarded as a supply chain question ('Looking at the entire supply chain, who should be doing what?') rather than a piecemeal outsource question ('Should we outsource this activity?').

Drivers for the growth of outsourcing:

- Quality drivers
- Cost drivers
- Business focus drivers
- Financial drivers
- Relationship drivers
- Human resource drivers

Advantages and disadvantages of strategic outsourcing

ADVANTAGES/BENEFITS	DISADVANTAGES/RISKS
Supports organisational rationalisation and downsizing	Potentially higher cost of services, contracting and management
Allows focused investment of managerial, staff and other resources on the organisation's core activities and competencies	Difficulty of ensuring service quality and consistency and corporate social responsibility
Accesses and leverages the specialist expertise, technology and resources of contractors	Potential loss of in-house expertise, knowledge, contacts or technologies
Access to economies of scale	Potential loss of control over key areas of performance and risk
Adds competitive performance incentives	Added distance from the customer or end-user
Leverages collaborative supply relationships	Risks of 'lock in' to an incompatible or under-performing relationship
Cost certainty	Risks of loss of control over confidential data and intellectual property
	Ethical and employee relations issues of transfer or cessation of activities
	Potential risks, costs and difficulties of in-sourcing if the outsource arrangement fails

Competencies and contractor competence

		COMPETENCE OF CONTRACTORS	
		High	Low
CORE IMPORTANCE	Low	Outsource/buy in	Develop contracting
	High	Collaboration	In-house

The supply chain management function may be particularly well placed to assess the implications of the 'buy' option, because it is familiar with the supply market; supplier capabilities, capacity and compatibility; and likely comparative costs.

Offshoring and low-cost country sourcing

Two main sources of advantage through internationalisation or offshoring:

- The exploitation of **locational advantages**
- The development of an **international value network**

Possible locational advantages in different overseas product and supply markets:

- Cost advantages: eg lower labour costs, lower logistics and transportation costs
- Local resources and competencies
- National or regional market characteristics

These sources of advantage may be exploited strategically in various ways.

- By entry into international product or service markets
- By accessing production capabilities through foreign direct investment and joint ventures ('offshoring') or outsourcing (discussed above)
- By international or global sourcing: procuring inputs, services and complementary competencies from strategic, value-adding suppliers – regardless of geographic location.

Advantages of international sourcing:

- Access to required materials, facilities and/or skills, which may not be available locally
- Availability of culturally distinctive goods
- Access to a wider supplier base
- Opportunities for cost savings
- Exchange rate advantages
- Competitive quality
- Reduced regulatory and compliance burden
- Leveraging available ICT developments
- Support for supply chain agility
- Ability to compete with competitors who are benefiting from any or all of the above advantages

Possible drawbacks:

- Socio-cultural differences
- Language barriers
- Legal issues
- Logistical and supply risks
- Exchange rate risk
- Payment risk
- Difficulties of monitoring and assuring quality, environmental and ethical standards in overseas supplier operations
- General STEEPLE factor risks in the overseas environment
- Additional sourcing costs

Sourcing from low-cost countries poses sustainability issues and risks, with the potential for exploitation of vulnerable suppliers and workers. For example, some countries may lack political or economic stability, compatible legal regimes, standards of quality, labour and human rights etc.

Quality improvement methodologies

Quality is a critical success factor for most businesses, because it determines customer satisfaction. Improved quality also:

- Adds economic value by allowing the organisation to charge premium prices – and
- Adds customer value by enhancing perceived product benefits.

The supply chain has a crucial role in maintaining, assuring and improving quality.

- At the operational level, this involves matters such as materials specification, early supplier involvement, service level agreements, contracting, supplier evaluation, quality control, benchmarking, contract management and so on.
- At a strategic level, this may involve strategic relationship management, supply chain and supplier development, total quality management and continuous improvement, and the establishment of systems for measuring and managing supply chain performance.

Two approaches to quality management:

- Reactive **defect detection** approaches such as inspection and quality control (QC)
- Proactive **defect prevention** approaches such as quality assurance (QA), statistical process control and total quality management. Quality assurance seeks to build quality into every stage of the process from concept and specification onwards.

The term **quality management** is given to all the various online and offline processes used to ensure that the right quality inputs and outputs are secured: that products and services are fit for purpose and conform to specification; and that continuous quality improvements are obtained over time. Quality management thus includes both quality control and quality assurance.

TQM is an extension and development of quality management thinking, with its emphasis on building quality into new products, services and processes from the beginning. TQM takes this a step further, to recognise explicitly that:

- Customers are the ultimate definers of value, and the ultimate drivers for delivering quality
- Quality management requires the design and management of processes to meet customer needs cost-effectively and competitively
- Quality management requires everyone in the organisation (and, increasingly, across the supply chain) to view everything in terms of meeting customer needs – and to be involved in meeting customer needs.

Key principles and values of a TQM approach:

- Focus on the customer
- Quality chains
- Quality culture
- Total involvement
- Quality through people
- Team-based management

- Get it right first time
- Process alignment
- Quality management systems
- Continuous improvement or *kaizen*
- Sharing best practice.

OWN NOTES

OWN NOTES

CHAPTER 3

The Impact of Market Change

The supply chain management environment

The environment of an organisation or strategic business unit can be seen as a series of concentric circles: internal environment; micro environment; and macro environment.

Three influences of the external environment on the organisation:

- It presents *threats* and *opportunities*.
- It is the source of *resources* needed by the organisation.
- It contains *stakeholders* who may seek, or have the right, to influence the activities of the organisation.

Steps in environmental analysis

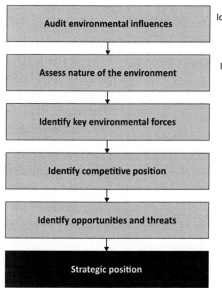

Audit environmental influences	Identify environmental factors that are affecting or might affect the organisation and its market.
Assess nature of the environment	Identify whether the environment is stable or changing (dynamic), and what the changes and trends are.
Identify key environmental forces	Identify which factors are having or will have the greatest impact on the organisation
Identify competitive position	Determine how the organisation stands compared to competitors for the same resources (eg by market share analysis).
Identify opportunities and threats	Identify opportunities or threats posed by the environment and how well the organisation's strategy and structure are matched to these.
Strategic position	

Procurement function's strategic role in appraising supply markets:

- Environmental analysis
- Industry analysis
- Competitor analysis
- Critical success factor analysis
- Supply, demand and capacity forecasting
- Vendor analysis
- Supply market analysis

STEEPLE factors and supply chains

The STEEPLE framework

FACTORS	EXAMPLES
Socio-cultural	Demographics; consumerism and consumer power; education and skilling infrastructure; values; attitudes to work, employment equity and employee relations; cultural differences; gender roles
Technological	ICT developments; automation
Economic	The economic strength and stability of the nation or industry; rates of inflation, interest and tax; in international supply markets: exchange rates, comparative wages and taxes, freedom of labour and capital movements, trade agreements etc.
Environmental (or 'ecological')	Consumer demand and public pressure for eco-friendly products and processes; law and regulation; emerging priorities re green 'issues'; the availability, scarcity and price of natural resources and commodities
Political	Government policies; grants and subsidies; political risk (eg political or civil unrest or war)
Legal	A wide range of law and regulation on issues such as: employment rights; workplace health and safety; etc
Ethical	Consumer demand for ethically sourced and produced goods and services; ethical codes and standards; ethical and reputational risk; the 'employer brand' of the organisation

Strategic planners need to identify, understand and target their strategies in relation to:

- Their direct competitors
- Their markets.

It may be helpful for an organisation to identify and analyse the **strategic groups** that represent their most direct, or comparable, competitors. This may help planners to:

- Identify the **most direct competitors** of the organisation
- Identify the **basis of competition** within the group
- Identify **opportunities and threats**

Supply chain management may be a distinguishing characteristic of a strategic group. For example:

- Some organisations may position themselves and compete on the basis of local sourcing while others compete on the benefits of international or global sourcing.
- One strategic group may compete on the basis of lean supply while another competes on the basis of agile supply.
- One strategic group may base its supply chain and sourcing strategies on lowest cost or cost reduction while another competes on the basis of sustainable, ethical and responsible sourcing and trading.
- One strategic group may seek to manage supply risk through strong control over the supply chain while another may focus on the flexibility and price advantages of opportunistic switching.

Market segmentation is defined as 'the process of dividing a potential market into distinct subsets of consumers with common needs or characteristics'. Small market segments may be identified as 'niches'. The term 'target marketing' is given to the process by which organisations segment their markets, decide which segments to aim for ('market targeting'), and develop a marketing mix (decisions about product, price, distribution and promotion) tailored to targeted segments ('product positioning').

The impact of market change

Organisations (and their supply chains) are subject to constant, often turbulent, environmental change and uncertainty. A wide range of STEEPLE factors may act as external triggers or drivers of strategic change.

The term **transformational (or revolutionary) change** is often given to a reactive approach, responding to 'disruptive' change in the environment, crisis or the need for a completely new paradigm. It seeks to overthrow (or throw out) the *status quo* and introduce radical transformation in a relatively short period of time.

Incremental (or evolutionary) change is often used as a proactive approach, building on the existing situation (the *status quo*) in small steps over a long period of time. This is the basis of business improvement strategies such as *kaizen* (continuous improvement) and total quality management. Benefits of incremental change:

- It builds on existing skills, routines and beliefs in the organisation.
- It allows flexibility and responsiveness to environmental changes and feedback, allowing constant re-alignment of strategy.
- It allows a continuous sense of progress, even through uncertainty and difficulty.
- It empowers employees.

JSW distinguish between emergent change and planned change.

- **Emergent change** is allowed to develop naturally, often from the bottom up, in response to environmental influences.

- **Planned change** involves deliberately-formulated strategies and programmes for implementing change.

JSW argue that the main problem posed for organisations by their environments is uncertainty, arising from complexity, dynamism and volatility.

- In a **complex** environment, there are a variety of influences which may impact on the organisation.
- In a **dynamic** environment, change is driven by significant and powerful forces.
- In a **volatile** or 'turbulent' environment, there is a high degree of instability.

Complex and volatile environments require a new set of core competencies from organisations: the ability to be flexible or adaptable, and to respond swiftly (and without trauma) to constant and perhaps unforeseeable change. Where conditions are dynamic or turbulent, the priority will be to make sense of an uncertain future – rather than simply extrapolating from the past. Managers will need to:

- Encourage proactive environmental scanning and feedback-seeking
- Utilise scenario planning techniques
- Develop organisation and supply chain structures and cultures for agility
- Encourage organisational and supply chain learning
- See strategy development in terms of logical incrementalism

Where conditions are complex and hard to comprehend, the emphasis may be on:

- Decentralising strategy development
- Developing capability for organisational learning and adaptation

The impact of globalisation

Globalisation is 'the increasing integration of internationally dispersed economic activities'. This may involve the globalisation of markets, production, and/or finance.

Drivers of globalisation:

- Improvements in transport technology
- Improvements in ICT
- Reduction in trade barriers
- Increasing numbers of multinational corporations
- Convergence in cultural values and consumer tastes
- The business benefits of larger markets, economies of scale, etc

Arguments in favour of globalisation:

- International trade stimulates local economic activity. This leads to improved productivity and output, and helps to create employment, leading to greater prosperity, educational development and other standard-of-living benefits.
- The siting of operations in developing countries may bring investment in technology, infrastructure, education and skill development which the host country could not afford on its own.

- There may be improvements in human rights and labour conditions.
- Global consumers benefit from more product and service choice and competitive pricing.
- International trade is a primary mechanism for positive international relations and a deterrent to conflict.

Arguments against globalisation:

- It encourages the exploitation of labour in developing nations.
- It encourages the exploitation of local markets.
- It 'exports' pollution and other environmental damage to developing nations.
- It undermines governments in the management of their own domestic economies
- It causes unemployment in developed nations.
- It squeezes small, local businesses out of markets, with negative effects on competition, communities and cultures.
- It encourages the homogenisation of cultures.

Drivers of change in globalised supply chains:

- Increased competition
- Drive for cost reduction
- Technology development
- Speed of new product development
- Diverse and changing customer demand
- 'Green' and ethical pressures
- Collaborations and joint ventures
- Global outsourcing

In response to the challenges of globalisation and complexity, companies are responding strategically by:

- Developing collaboration initiatives with suppliers
- Integrating partner-facing collaboration processes with internal business processes
- Developing collaboration initiatives with customers
- Refreshing and integrating enabling technologies.

Assessing supply chain risk

Stages in the risk management cycle: identify sources of risk; assess probability and impact of potential risks; formulate risk management strategies and contingency plans; allocate accountabilities and resources; implement risk management strategies; monitor, report and adjust.

Techniques for **identifying** supply chain risks: environmental scanning; formal risk analysis exercises; critical incident investigations; process audits; consulting with stakeholders and industry experts; employing third-party risk management consultants.

Risk **assessment** is the appraisal of the probability and significance of identified potential risk events: in other words, asking 'how likely is it and how bad could it be?' Risk is commonly assessed as a function of:

- The *likelihood* that an element of risk, or risk event, will occur and
- The *impact* (or consequences) that will result if it does occur (both positive and negative – although negative or 'downside' impacts are most often the focus).

Another technique that may be used for risk identification and assessment is the **mapping** of the supply chain or value stream.

Scenario analysis involves:

- Using brainstorming or facilitated group workshops to stimulate the identification of issues and possibilities
- Describing or computer-modelling the key variables in a scenario
- Altering selected variables and observing the effect
- Creating best, most likely and worst case scenarios to measure impacts.

Risk management strategies ('what can we do about it?') – the Four Ts:

- *Tolerate* (or accept) the risk
- *Transfer* or spread the risk
- *Terminate* (or avoid) the risk
- *Treat* (or mitigate) the risk

Some strategic sourcing options appear inherently risky: supply base rationalisation; development of lean and agile supply chains; global sourcing and offshoring.

However, it is generally acknowledged that effective SCM may help to reduce risk and supply chain vulnerability in the following ways.

- Encouraging the proactive monitoring, identification and assessment of supply chain, supplier and supply market risks
- Providing greater end-to-end supply chain data sharing, transparency and visibility
- Supporting greater transparency and trust in individual supplier relationships
- Improving security and continuity of supply
- Promoting the intentional and rigorous selection of long-term strategic supply chain partners, with risk management capabilities a key qualification criterion
- Promoting the effective management of contracts, suppliers and supplier performance
- Encouraging systems integration and joint development
- Encouraging supply chain mapping and analysis
- Creating improved end-to-end supply chain visibility

OWN NOTES

3

OWN NOTES

CHAPTER 4

Strategic Relationship Management

Supply chain relationships

Transactional vs relationship approaches to supply chain dealings

TRANSACTIONAL	RELATIONSHIP
Focus on sourcing lowest-price or best-value suppliers for one-off purchase transactions	Focus on retaining and developing value-adding, competitive-advantage-giving suppliers
Short timescale; operational orientation	Longer-term timescale; strategic orientation
Arm's length, impersonal dealings	Aim for collaboration, trust and mutual commitment
Low level of contact and communication	High level of contact and communication
Primary concern with effective supplier outputs	Primary concern with effective collaborative processes

The relationship spectrum: at one end there are **competitive** relationships, in which buyer and supplier compete for share of value. At the other end there are **collaborative** relationships, in which buyer and supplier work together for mutual benefit. There are various versions of the spectrum, often relying on concepts such as 'core competencies' and 'strategic alignment', which are central to effective supply chain management.

Factors determining the most appropriate relationship type:

- The nature and importance of the items being sourced
- The competence, capability, co-operation and performance of suppliers
- Geographical distance
- The compatibility of the supply partners
- The organisation's and supply chain management function's objectives and priorities
- Supply market conditions
- Legal and regulatory requirements

Benefits of close supply relationships: sound risk management; better return on relationship investment; improved business efficiency; greater profitability; potential for synergy; improved management of CSR, sustainability and reputational issues; competitive advantage.

Customer relationship management

Managing customer relationships today offers opportunities that go far beyond cost containment. Different types of end-customers:

- Business customers are fewer in number, but purchase at higher volumes and values.
- Their needs are generally more specialised and complex, and their buying more professional.
- Because of this, industrial buyer-supplier relationships tend to be more long-term and partnership-oriented.

It is crucial for supply chain professionals to view their role in the context of an internal supply chain: the **internal customer concept**.

One of the practical applications of relationship marketing is the discipline of **customer relationship management** (or CRM): the process of analysing, planning and managing relationships, with the particular goal of focusing both marketing and supply chain strategies on more profitable customers.

E-CRM is the use of electronic channels to market to, sell to and serve customers, both directly and with channel partners. Internet-enabled customer service offers a range of benefits.

- High-reach, low-cost communication with customers
- The ability to capture customer data
- Managed interactions with customers
- Facilitation of 'word-of-mouth' promotion
- Customer empowerment and decision facilitation
- The ability to complete one-stop integrated transactions through electronic payment systems.

Intermediaries are a distinct sub-set of customers. Relationship management still applies, but there are some distinctive features arising from the fact that channel intermediaries are *businesses,* and occupy a special role in the supply chain.

Supplier relationship management

One of the ways positive supplier relationships can be leveraged for supply chain improvement and competitiveness is by 'broadening supply'. This has some advantages (eg, arguably, in reducing risk).

More commonly, strong collaborative supplier relationships are used to 'narrow supply', enabling purchases to be concentrated on a smaller group of developed and trusted supply partners. **Supplier base rationalisation** (or optimisation) is concerned with determining roughly how many suppliers the buying firm wants to do business with.

However, a very narrow supplier base opens the buyer to risks: over-dependence on a few suppliers; supply disruption; loss of preferred suppliers' goodwill; preferred suppliers growing complacent; being locked in to under-performing suppliers; missing out on more competitive suppliers.

Benefits of supplier relationship management:

- Identifying operational improvement opportunities, both supplier-side *and* buyer-side
- Generating cost-reduction opportunities
- Driving innovation
- Enhancing customer focus and insight
- Embedding responsibility for delivery of improvements and customer benefits at an operational level
- Systematically encouraging longer-term, supply-chain thinking

Implementing SRM – four phases:

- Identify targets within the procurement portfolio for cost savings
- Collaboratively develop a detailed view of the relevant operational performance issues across the supply chain
- Collaboratively identify and prioritise the areas on which the SRM will focus
- Jointly commit to a co-ordinated program of action to achieve the intended results.

Collaborative planning

Vendor managed inventory (VMI) is a collaboration replenishment approach, under which vendors are given: (a) access to information (production plans, ordering, sales forecasts) and (b) delegated responsibility for managing and replenishing the buyer's inventory, within policy guidelines. Such stocks as need to be carried are mostly held on the vendor's premises.

Collaborative planning, forecasting and replenishment (CPFR) is a more radical process for day-to-day category management. It involves the collaborative sharing of information on customer demand (sales), across the supply chain, with the aim of collaborative planning (joint sales and order forecasting), to support efficient replenishment – with the aim of mutual gains in profitability for all parties.

Because of the emphasis on the sharing of demand information, CPFR demands robust disciplines for data accuracy, integrity and integration *within* each partner organisation, as a foundation for collaborative forecasting.

Partnership sourcing

When might partnership be beneficial?

- Where the customer has a high spend with the supplier
- Where the customer faces high risk
- Where the product supplied is technically complex
- Where the product is vital and complex

- Where the supply market for the product is fast-changing
- In a restricted supply market

Characteristics of partnership sourcing:

- Cultural compatibility between the partners
- A high level of trust, knowledge sharing and openness
- Mutual acceptance of the concept of win-win within the supply chain
- Relevant expertise, resources or competencies in complementary areas
- Clear joint objectives and meaningful performance measures for assessing supply chain performance
- The use of cross-functional teams
- A total quality management philosophy
- A high degree of systems integration

Supplier development

Supplier development is: 'Any activity that a buyer undertakes to improve a supplier's performance and/or capabilities to meet the buyer's short-term or long-term supply needs'.

Two main types of supplier development: results-oriented development; process-oriented development.

Responsibilities and roles in supplier development can be structured in various ways.

- Supplier development programmes will often involve **cross-functional representatives**.
- Communication systems will probably provide for **multiple contact points**.
- Another common practice is the temporary **transfer of staff**.
- To further reinforce the interface with key suppliers some organisations have introduced the role of **executive sponsors**.

Two generic approaches to supplier development programmes: directive and facilitative.

Given the appropriate degree of market influence, a directive approach can be effective. A more relational or facilitative approach requires more effort and investment, and may therefore be used for strategic relationships and improvements.

If you had to pick five steps to describe this process (which might be more realistic for discussion in an exam), you might boil the programme down to: identifying critical products; appraising supplier performance and identifying performance gaps; forming a cross-functional SD team; negotiating improvements and deadlines; and monitoring performance.

Approaches to bridge perceived performance or relationship gaps:

- Enhancing working relationships
- Clarifying or increasing performance goals and measures
- Seconding purchaser's staff to the supplier (or *vice versa*)
- Providing capital

- Providing progress payments during the development of a project or product, to support the supplier's cashflow
- Loaning machinery, equipment or IT hardware
- Granting access to ICT systems and information
- Using the purchaser's bargaining power to obtain materials or equipment for the supplier at a discount
- Offering training for the supplier's staff in relevant areas
- Providing help or consultancy on value analysis (waste reduction) programmes, costing or other areas of expertise
- Encouraging the formation of industry-level collaborative mechanisms such as supplier forums

Costs and benefits of supplier development activities

BUYER'S PERSPECTIVE	
COSTS	BENEFITS
Cost of management time in researching, identifying and negotiating opportunities	Support for outsourcing strategies
Cost of development activities and resources	Improved products and services
Costs of ongoing relationship management	Streamlining systems and processes
Risks of sharing information and intellectual property	Gaining discounts or other benefits as a *quid pro quo* for development
SUPPLIER'S PERSPECTIVE	
COSTS	BENEFITS
Cost of management time in researching, identifying and negotiating opportunities	Support for production and process efficiencies and cost savings
Cost of development	Improvements in customer service and satisfaction
Costs of ongoing relationship management	Improved capacity and service levels
Risks of sharing information and intellectual property	Direct gains in knowledge and resources provided by the customer
Cost of discounts or exclusivity agreements	Enhanced learning and flexibility

OWN NOTES

CHAPTER 5

Supply Chain Segmentation

Supply chain market alignment

Portfolio analysis and segmentation involves categorising and dividing the firm's customers (and/or products and services) and suppliers (and/or procurement portfolio) into different classes, according to relevant criteria such as volume and value of business, profitability, market complexity and risk – or, broadly, 'importance' to the firm's strategic objectives. The segment into which a given supplier falls indicates the purchasing resources, sourcing approach and relationship type that will be most important, as a basis for sourcing and relationship action plans. Similarly, the segment into which a given customer falls indicates the marketing and distribution resources, approach and relationship type that will optimise value.

Portfolio segmentation on the upstream side (**supplier segmentation**) allows the supply chain function to:

- Focus and leverage available resources, while minimising identified supply and supplier risk factors
- Follow a standardised framework for decision-making and action planning in regard to portfolio management of supplies and suppliers
- Justify portfolio management decisions on the basis of robust criteria and analysis.

Customer segmentation

A market consists of both current and potential customers with the ability to buy a product or service. Market segmentation is 'the process of dividing a potential market into distinct subsets of consumers with common needs or characteristics'.

Customer segmentation has long been used by sales and marketing professionals, based on classification of customer characteristics: demographic and psychographic factors; media and channel preferences; geographic location; B2C or B2B markets.

Supply chain segmentation is based on an assessment of how buyer values have an impact on the way they interact with the supply chain. *Supply chain segments help to identify the types of supply chains required to respond to customer needs.*

Supply chain segmentation may be developed using a 'buyer value framework' to map customers against buyer value descriptions. Gattorna uses the **PADI** classification and description ('taxonomy') of buyer values.

Managing the product/service mix

Basic descriptions of segment characteristics can be refined to incorporate:

- The nature of the demand (eg evenness of demand, stability, predictability)
- Buyer values (eg urgent delivery requirements, focus on price opportunism, loyalty and so on)

This information can be used to identify key operating characteristics or guiding principles for managing the segment – which in turn can be used to define an appropriate strategic response.

The Ansoff matrix (marketing)   *Adapted for wider strategic choice*

	Existing product	*New product*		*Existing product*	*New product*
New market	**Market development**	**Diversification**	**New market**	**Market development** New segments New territories New uses	**Diversification** On existing competencies With new competencies
Existing market	**Market penetration**	**Product development**	**Existing market**	**Market penetration** Withdrawal Consolidation Market penetration	**Product development** On existing competencies With new competencies

Key strategic choices:

- **Withdrawal** may be desirable if the organisation has been unable to develop sufficient resources and competencies.
- **Consolidation** is a strategy of protecting and perhaps strengthening the organisation's position in its existing markets.
- **Market penetration** is a growth strategy, based on gaining greater market share in an existing market, with an existing product.
- **Product development** is a growth strategy, based on introducing new (or modified or complementary) products to existing markets.
- **Market development** is a growth strategy, based on finding new markets for existing products.
- **Diversification** involves the development of new products for new markets.

Portfolio matrices are a range of tools and models which can be used by managers to make decisions about strategic priorities within and across their business portfolio: that is, about which SBUs and products or services to invest in. The Boston Consulting Group (BCG) matrix is one of the most popular and influential methods for analysing the strength and balance of a portfolio of products. It maps them on two dimensions: market share and market growth.

The strategies for the overall portfolio are generally concerned with balance. Objectives might include:

- Development of cash cows of sufficient size and/or number to support other areas of the portfolio (eg investment in question marks)
- Development of stars of sufficient size and/or number to provide future cash cows
- Nurturing of clusters of stars with reasonable prospects of becoming future stars
- Disinvestment from dogs, or creation of a good business case for retaining them.

Supplier segmentation

Reasons why a supplier might be strategically significant:

- If they supply items which are strategic or critical to the effective performance of business processes, or to the manufacturer's product and brand
- If there are few suppliers in the market
- If they supply rare, distinctive, hard-to-imitate, value-adding competencies
- If contracts with them represent a significant proportion of the buying organisation's external spend
- If their resources and competencies mitigate significant downside supply risks
- If there is potential for significant synergy
- If significant investment has already been made in partnership and relationship-specific adaptations and assets

Strategic suppliers warrant significant investment in relationship and performance management and development – whereas operational suppliers generally do not.

Supplier relationships may also be classified and prioritised using more analytical tools such as: Pareto analysis; the Kraljic matrix; supplier preferencing.

The Pareto principle (or '80/20 rule') is a useful technique for identifying the activities that will leverage buyers' time, effort and resources for the biggest benefits. It is a popular way of prioritising between tasks or areas of focus. In the context of supply or supplier positioning, the Pareto principle can be interpreted as 80% of spend being directed towards just 20% of the suppliers.

Peter Kraljic (1983) developed a tool of analysis that seeks to map two factors.

- The **importance** to the organisation of the item or category being purchased
- The **complexity** of the supply market

Looking at the four quadrants:

- For **non-critical or routine items**, the focus will be on low-maintenance routines to reduce procurement costs.
- For **bottleneck items**, the buyer's priority will be ensuring control over the continuity and security of supply.
- For **leverage items**, the buyer's priority will be to use its dominance to secure best prices and terms, on a purely transactional basis.

- For **strategic items**, there is likely to be mutual dependency and investment.

The supplier preferencing model is another matrix, this time illustrating how attractive it is to a supplier to deal with a buyer, and the monetary value of the buyer's business to the supplier.

Supply chain tiering

There is a trade-off between the desire to minimise the costs and complexity of managing a large supplier network and the desire to minimise the risks of having a very narrow supplier base (creating vulnerability through dependency on a small number of suppliers). One of the solutions to this trade-off lies in the way the supply chain is structured: specifically, in the development of supply chain tiering.

Potential reasons for tiering suppliers:

- The top-level purchaser wants to develop partnerships with key suppliers, but only has time and resources to develop a limited number of such relationships.
- More and better supply chain improvements and innovations may be available from sharing information and collaborating with expert first-tier suppliers.
- Top-level procurement staff may be freed up to pursue a more strategic focus.

Key issues in developing different relationship and sourcing strategies to suit different tiers:

- The sourcing, selection and contracting of the first-tier suppliers will be a crucial strategic exercise.
- There will be fewer commercial relationships to manage at the first tier.
- The top-tier organisation will still need to 'drill down' through the tiers.
- The buyer may exercise influence over the first-tier supplier to adopt some of its own existing suppliers as subcontractors or lower-tier suppliers.

OWN NOTES

5

OWN NOTES

CHAPTER 6

Networked and Value-Adding Supply Chains

Supply chains and networks

A supply chain is 'that network of organisations that are involved, through upstream and downstream linkages, in the different processes and activities that produce value in the form of products and services in the hands of the ultimate customer'.

Drivers of this strategic perspective: cost pressures; reduced lead times; increased demand for quality.

Using the analogy or metaphor of a 'chain' highlights useful characteristics.

- It emphasises 'serial co-operation'.
- It emphasises mutual dependency and collaboration.
- It emphasises 'linkages' or interfaces between members.
- It is continuous and non-directional.

Many writers now argue that a more appropriate metaphor for the supply process is not a chain, but a network or web – which allows a more complex set of interrelated relationships and transactions to be depicted.

Seeing the supply chain as a network is helpful for a number of reasons.

- It is a more strategic model for mapping and analysing supply chain relationships.
- It raises the possibility of a wider range of collaborations.
- It represents both 'nodes' and the links between them.
- It recognises the potential of 'extended enterprises' and virtual organisations.
- It recognises that extended enterprises may overlap.

Three major challenges of supply networks:

- The need to view strategy development as a collective process
- The need to develop win-win thinking
- The need for open communication

Value and added value

From an **accounting perspective** added value is total revenue *minus* total cost of all activities undertaken to develop and market a product or service. An organisation can add value by:

- Inducing customers to pay more *and/or*
- Reducing costs or increasing the efficiency of processes.

From a **marketing perspective**, adding value means enhancing the offering to customers.

Porter's value chain

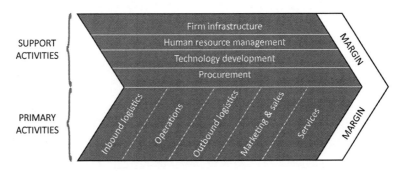

A firm must also secure competitive advantage by managing the *linkages within its supply network:* the basis of techniques such as lean and agile supply, total quality management and supply chain management. This wider value chain, extended through the supply chain, is known as a **value system** or **value network.**

Value-adding strategies that have emerged as a result of supply-chain thinking: value engineering; lean supply; agile supply; value-adding supply network relationships.

Porter argued that the development of linkages can often lead to competitive advantage via (a) optimisation and (b) co-ordination.

Activities and processes which add cost, without adding value, are identified as 'waste' activities. They contribute nothing to the flow of value to the customer – and should therefore be minimised or eliminated throughout the supply chain where possible.

The concept of repositioning an organisation within the supply or value chain implies the extension of its operations or control to a wider range of upstream or downstream activities – and a greater share of responsibility for creating and adding value.

- Organic or internal development and diversification into activities one step up or down the chain
- Acquisition of, or merger with, organisations one step up or down the chain
- Strategic collaboration and integration with organisations one step up or down the chain.

Value analysis in supply chains

Supply chain flows: the term 'process flow' is often used to describe the sequence of processes and activities that are performed to produce a desired outcome or result: for example, flows of information or materials and work in progress from one process stage to the next.

Supply chain mapping is a tool of analysis and communication, enabling managers to identify:

- Strong and weak linkages in the value chain
- Potential areas of supply risk
- Potential areas of sustainability, compliance or reputational risk
- Potential areas of opportunity or strength
- Areas of inefficiency in the supply chain
- Potential efficiencies
- The breakdown of costs, added value and profit at each stage of the supply chain
- Areas in which improved information or resource flows are required
- Weakness in reverse logistics, or lack of a closed loop supply chain
- Areas in which the organisation may need to move from a 'chain' to a 'network'.

Value stream mapping is another tool of process visualisation and communication. Its aim is to **identify, demonstrate and decrease waste** in supply and manufacturing processes. VSM involves mapping all key activities in the manufacturing process, with cycle times, down times, in-process inventory, material moves and information flows.

Value chain analysis identifies potential for the elimination of wastes and the addition of further value at various points and activities in the value chain.

- Identifying sub-activities for each primary activity and support activity
- Identifying linkages
- Looking for opportunities to increase value

A simplified three-stage approach to value chain analysis: activity analysis; value analysis; evaluation and planning.

Supply chain network optimisation modelling (NOM) is a technique for improving supply chain cost-efficiency and managing supply chain risk, using computer software to:

- Describe and measure all the activities in a complex supply chain network, *in order to*
- Select the optimal mix of strategies for materials sourcing, network infrastructure, processing activity and flows throughout the chain, *in order to*
- Minimise total costs, while staying within existing facility, process and logistics capacities and constraints, *in the light of*
- Varying estimates of future demand, costs, capacity and other internal and external factors.

Basic domains covered by an NOM model: raw materials sourcing; manufacturing/processing; demand fulfilment.

Network sourcing

Characteristics of network sourcing

CHARACTERISTIC	EXPLANATION
A tiered supply structure	The supply chain is a 'pyramid'
A small number of direct suppliers	Customers typically have few suppliers, and suppliers typically have few customers
High degrees of asset specificity	'Asset specificity' refers to the willingness of suppliers to make relationship-specific investments
A 'maximum buy' strategy by each company within the semi-permanent supplier network, but a 'maximum make' strategy within the network as a whole	Each participant in the network seeks to buy out (rather than make) as much as possible of its needs, sourcing from network partners. However, the network as a whole seeks to make as much as possible, minimising recourse to external suppliers.
A high degree of co-operative design and value engineering	Network partners work together to develop competitive offerings
A high degree of supplier innovation in new products and processes	Suppliers are willing to suggest and develop technically innovative improvements, for mutual benefit.
Close, long-term relations between network members	This involves a high level of trust, openness (data and knowledge sharing) and profit and gain sharing.
The use of rigorous supplier grading systems	Mutual commitment and high levels of performance
A high level of supplier coordination by the customer company	Customer companies develop and support co-ordinatory mechanisms
A significant effort made by customers at each of these levels to develop their suppliers	Co-operative circles and other mechanisms are used for knowledge and best practice sharing, technology transfer and other tools of supplier development.

Network sourcing (like lean supply) is a 'best practice' model which claims to be comprehensive, widely applicable and capable of optimising buyer-supplier relationships: its proponents argue that all firms should take a similarly structured approach to procurement and supply. Just as in general management and organisation theory, however, a 'contingency approach' has developed in response to the increasing complexity and dynamism of business environments.

An overall supply network perspective is significant, because it highlights three important design decisions.

- How should the network be configured?
- Where should each part of the network owned by the organisation be located?
- What physical capability should each part of the network owned by the company have?

Reverse logistics

Two principal drivers of interest in reverse logistics:

- The increased importance attached to the environmental aspects of waste disposal
- Recognition of the potential returns that can be obtained from the re-use of products or parts, or the recycling of materials.

Reasons for product returns:

- Customer not satisfied
- Installation or usage problems creating dissatisfaction
- Warranty claims
- Faulty order processing and fulfilment
- Retail overstock
- End of product lifecycle or product replacement
- Manufacturer product recalls
- Increasing patterns of consumer returns following e-commerce sales

Management issues in closed-loop supply chains:

- Effective supply base management, integration and collaboration
- Effective supplier and customer relationships
- Supplier selection and contract award on the basis of recycling or ecologically friendly disposal capacity
- Product and packaging design to facilitate return, recycling and safe disposal
- Visibility
- Reverse logistical activities
- Potential to create profit centres around reverse logistics and returns processes
- Potential to outsource the returns and reverse logistics process
- Challenges of unplanned-for product recalls
- Root-cause analysis, to identify quality and fulfilment problems resulting in product returns, repairs and recalls

6

OWN NOTES

CHAPTER 7

Distribution Systems

The role of distribution systems

Value-adding contributions of downstream channel members: assembly; storage and delivery; selling, advertising, promotion, display and merchandising; customer service and order processing; warranties and insurances; customer feedback and intelligence gathering and reporting.

Stages in the strategic distribution planning process:

- Developing a thorough understanding and appreciation of business strategies and marketing plans, as the basis for balancing cost and service effectiveness
- Evaluating customer (segment) service requirements to determine what elements are viewed as key
- Analysing the distribution system and the total costs of production and distribution

At a strategic level, distribution planning concerns issues such as:

- Channels of distribution
- The type, size and location of depots, warehouses and distribution centres
- Inventory policy
- The application of information and communication technology to transport planning, facility design, materials handling, inventory management and so on
- The potential for third- or fourth-party outsourcing

Channel design

Strategic decisions in channel management:

- Whether to distribute direct to the customer or via intermediaries
- What types of distributor should be used for each value creation element
- How many of each type
- How specific intermediaries should be selected and managed.

Major determinants of channel design:

- The characteristics of the product or service
- The characteristics of the customer segment
- The organisation's value proposition
- The capabilities and value-adding activities required to deliver the value proposition

- The determination of which types of intermediary partners will be in the best position to provide complementary capabilities, and at what cost
- The optimal channel structure to deliver the value proposition competitively

Intermediary options: wholesalers; distributors and dealers; agents; franchisees; retailers.

- To facilitate direct marketing and relationship marketing
- To eliminate physical distribution for some products and services
- To facilitate virtual supply chains
- To globalise supply chains
- To facilitate customer empowerment
- To support supply chain integration and collaboration
- To offer improved supply chain management solutions

Logistics flow path design

Logistics flow paths can be configured on the basis of:

- Differentiated service levels to be offered to meet the needs of different customer segments cost-effectively
- The division of the product portfolio into groups, on the basis of a shared logistics service proposition
- Optimisation of the number and location of plants and distribution centres

The main factors shaping logistics flow path design.

- Logistics operational complexity
- Customer logistics sophistication
- The organisation's industry, target market(s) and product/service portfolio
- The organisation's supply/value chain positioning

Physical network configuration

'Physical network configuration' involves decisions about:

- The types of plants, warehouses, stores or distribution centres required
- The levels of distribution facilities required
- The configuration of distribution hubs and spokes
- The numbers and locations of manufacturing and distribution centres required
- The identification of which customer and product groups will be served from each facility
- The appropriate level of inventory for each node in the network
- The transportation modes to be used for each linkage in the network
- Whether some or all of the network might be outsourced

Two main purposes of distribution centres: breaking bulk; consolidating deliveries.

Factors in the location of warehouses and distribution centres:

- Length of transport lines from the location to key customers
- Proximity and ease of access to major transportation hubs and routes

- Convenience, cost-effectiveness and environmental and social impacts
- Cost of space, facilities and infrastructure development
- The availability and flexibility of local labour and skills
- Environmental and social impacts of the facility, and stakeholder acceptability

Inbound logistics facilities and services from 3PL operators:

- Warehousing, including inventory management, inspection and so on
- Consolidation of consignments for inbound freight
- Breaking bulk and transport to different user sites
- Satellite (GPS) tracking and tracing of goods in transit
- Sophisticated transport (route and load) planning
- Unitisation of loads (providing pallets and containers)
- Transport fleet management
- Freight forwarding
- Accurate cost estimates for collection and transport of overseas supplies

Transportation management

Core competencies for effective inbound and outbound logistics:

- Understanding the fundamentals of transportation
- Embracing the concept of *integrated transportation management*
- Having capabilities to operationalise the vision and strategy for integrated transportation

Factors in the choice of transport mode:

- The points of departure and destination, for which limited options may be available
- The length of journey, raising issues of lead time, risk and cost
- The nature of the goods
- Timescale and urgency of customer delivery expectations
- The environmental impact of different modes of transport
- Availability of standardisation (eg of container sizes)
- Customers' goods inwards facilities
- The security of goods in transit
- The costs of transport, handling and insurance
- The optimal mix of modes and transitions to achieve service and price objectives

Challenges in transportation management at a strategic level:

- Long-term strategic planning
- Co-ordination of inbound transportation from vendors with other transportation activities
- Deciding which parties in the supply network should control freight operations
- Deciding the optimal mix of transportation modes
- Managing inbound delivery economics
- The development and acquisition of suitable enabling technology
- Fleet ownership

- Fleet management
- The management of transport security and other risks

International or global distribution raises additional issues and risks:

- The need to use intermodal transport
- Variations in transport infrastructure and availability of different modes of transport
- The length (in time and distance) of the journey
- Different customs jurisdictions
- Multiple contracts involved in securing delivery
- Different legal jurisdictions
- Communication and language difficulties

Positioning in local, regional and global chains

Ogulin's matrix: 'For companies, the significance of capabilities in a local versus regional and global context is to analyse capabilities relative to other companies in their industry'. In other words, they need to *position* themselves within the global supply chain arena.

Positioning in local, regional and global supply chains

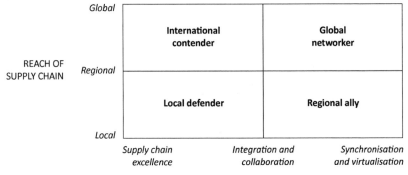

BREADTH AND DEPTH OF SUPPLY CHAIN CAPABILITY

OWN NOTES

OWN NOTES

CHAPTER 8

Lean and Agile Supply Chains

Lean thinking and lean supply

'Lean production is "lean" because it uses less of every thing compared with mass production: half the human effort in the factory, half the factory space ... The expected results are fewer defects, while producing a greater and ever growing variety of products' (Krafcik).

Five key principles to lean thinking:

- Specify what creates value as seen from the customer's perspective
- Identify all steps across the value stream
- Make actions that create value 'flow'
- Only make what is pulled by customer demand, just in time
- Strive for perfection by continually removing successive layers of waste

Structural and cultural features of lean organisations:

- Decentralisation of tasks and responsibilities
- Control systems based on discovering defects and problems immediately, and eliminating their causes
- Comprehensive integrated information systems to enable swift and flexible response
- Horizontal organisation based on empowered cross-functional teams
- A strong sense of mutual loyalty between employees and the organisation

Ohno's seven wastes: over-production; transportation; waiting; motion; over-processing; inventory; defects/corrections.

Lean supply is: 'the elimination of duplication of effort and capability in the supply chain, combined with a philosophy of continuously increasing the expectations of performance and self-imposed pressure to excel.' Lean supply networks collaborate intentionally, in order to progressively eliminate cost and waste (at any and all points of the supply chain), with the overall goal of optimising the customer value stream.

JIT supply is a radical Japanese approach to inventory reduction which aims to ensure that inputs only arrive at the factory (and particular work stations in the assembly line) 'just in time' to go into the production process. Like lean production, JIT focuses on waste-eliminating measures. The core philosophy of JIT is that 'inventory is evil'.

8

Key performance objectives of JIT: quality; speed; flexibility; dependability.

Limitations and risks to JIT as a supply chain strategy:

- Gains are offset by some reduction in capacity utilisation, loss of economies of scale, and additional transport costs.
- Gains come at a risk (no time or stock buffers)
- There may be additional costs associated with the evaluation, development and management of high-quality, long-term supply partners
- 'The introduction of 'just-in-time' delivery may reduce inventory in the factory, but increase it at the supplier.'
- Buyers may pay a higher unit price to compensate for the supplier's costs in supplying on a JIT basis.

Similar issues with lean supply: many benefits are claimed, but there are also downsides.

Agile supply

'Agility is concerned primarily with responsiveness. It is about the ability to match supply and demand in turbulent and unpredictable markets. In essence, it is about being demand-driven rather than forecast-driven'.

Achieving agility may require:

- Streamlining the physical flow of parts from suppliers
- Streamlining and synchronising the flow of information
- Adaptability in responding to changing needs of the market
- Exploring the potential of specialist 4PL providers
- Measuring the performance of the supply chain using suitable agility metrics
- Recognising that supply chain managers are also 'change managers'.

Distinction between lean and agile:

- **Lean:** having no surplus flesh or bulk (powerful when the winning criteria are cost and quality). Lean manufacturing aims to produce goods only when 'pulled' by a customer (just in time) and to the standard of quality required by the customer.
- **Agile:** quick in movement, nimble (powerful when the winning criteria are service and customer value enhancement). Agile manufacturing, by means of postponement and/or late customisation, aims to *finish or assemble* goods in rapid response to customer orders – and, in the case of late customisation, to customer specification.

It is possible to combine the benefits of lean and agile in a hybrid system sometimes known as 'leagility'. One 'hybrid' solution is to utilise lean principles when developing the supply chains for standard products with stable demand and long lead times, and agile principles for the supply of unpredictable 'special' products with volatile demand and short lead times.

Another approach is to separate or **decouple** business processes at a particular point: in this case, the point in the supply chain where the customer order penetrates the system.

Processes upstream of this point are planned on lean principles, to maximise operational efficiency. Processes downstream of this point are planned on agile principles, for swift and flexible responsiveness to customer requirements.

Matching supply and demand

Just-in-time, lean and agile supply – and, more generally, efficient demand and capacity management – depend to a large extent on the ability to forecast demand. Unfortunately, demand forecasting is not an exact science, particularly over the long term.

Determinants of demand:

- Demand for the final product into which the purchased materials and components are incorporated (dependent demand)
- Demand for purchased finished items, such as office equipment and supplies, computer hardware and software or maintenance services (independent demand)
- The inventory policy of the organisation
- The service level required
- Market conditions
- Supply-side factors

Sales, marketing and promotional activities are explicitly intended to stimulate demand. Sales promotions, in particular, are intended to stimulate short-term demand and sales. Effective promotional activity is likely to have an immediate impact on the product promoted, during the time-frame of the promotion. However, there may also be indirect impacts.

Other influences on demand:

- Competitor promotional activity
- Third-party promotional activity
- The introduction of new products
- The discontinuation of a product or format
- Prices rising or falling in a market
- Economic and industry cycles
- A variety of macro-economic factors

One final problem: amplification of demand along the supply chain (the bullwhip effect or Forrester effect).

Improving demand planning accuracy

Githens emphasises that 'the ability to generate an accurate demand plan starts with the ability to generate a valid forecast'. He suggests steps for improving accuracy in demand planning: statistical forecasting; promotions management; causal event management; demand plan integration; reduced variability.

Predictions about demand are generally made by using:

- Historical data (eg on sales, or usage)
- Current data and information (such as that available from sales and production records, and suppliers)
- Market research and environmental monitoring.

Statistical techniques for forecasting demand: simple moving average; weighted average (or exponential smoothing); time series analysis; regression analysis.

Statistical methods are unlikely to be able to take into account all the various environmental factors which may cause fluctuations in demand. A number of more subjective or 'qualitative' methods may therefore be used, based on the knowledge, experience and judgement of expert buyers, suppliers, consultants or other stakeholders.

- Marketing and/or customer research can be used to ascertain potential interest and demand, particularly in new products.
- Expert opinion is the gathering of views, judgements and opinions from people regarded as knowledgeable and experienced in relevant business areas, markets and disciplines (such as consumer behaviour).
- The Delphi method seeks to add some objectivity and statistical rigour to the gathering of expert opinion.

Technology and supply chain communication

The contribution of ICT to supply chain communication and integration – with the potential to support:

- Improved end-to-end visibility of demand and supply within the supply chain
- Improved demand planning, demand management and capacity management throughout the supply chain
- Improved risk management
- Supply chain responsiveness and agility.

ICT-enabled supply chain communication is central to the four key characteristics of truly agile supply chains.

- Market sensitivity
- Virtual supply chains
- Process alignment
- Network sourcing

An **intranet** is a set of networked and/or internet-linked computers. This private network is usually only accessible to registered users, within the same organisation or work group. Access is restricted by passwords and user group accounts, for example. Intranets are used in internal supply chain and employee communication.

An **extranet** is an intranet that has been extended to give selected external partners (such as suppliers) authorised access to particular areas or levels of the organisation's website or information network, for exchanging data and applications, and sharing information.

Supply-chain-focused extranets usually provide suppliers with:

- Real-time access to inventory and demand information
- Authorised report information eg their vendor rating analysis

Extranet systems provide potential for removing process costs and increasing supply chain communication, real-time information-sharing, co-ordination and responsiveness (eg for improved demand management and just in time supply).

The term 'e-sourcing' is used for the processes and tools involved in 'using the internet to make decisions and form strategies regarding how and where services or products are obtained' (CIPS).

Potential benefits of developing e-sourcing:

- Reduced costs through increased process efficiencies, reduced sourcing costs, improvements in contract performance management etc.
- Best practice development
- Enhanced quality and capability
- Reduced sourcing cycle times
- Enhanced internal collaboration
- Improved training and efficiency
- Strategic focus

Risks and costs of technology leverage:

- High capital investment and set-up costs
- High initial learning curve costs
- Reliability issues, especially at an early stage of development
- Compatibility issues, if the system is required to work together with the different systems of suppliers
- Ethical issues, such as forcing smaller suppliers to invest in collaborative technologies
- Data security risks

OWN NOTES

CHAPTER 9

Collaborative Supply Chain Management

Supply chain evolution

Trends in supply chain evolution:

- Development towards total strategic integration of supply chain management with the major lines of business
- Development towards co-ordinated or 'centre led' procurement and supply chain management
- Development from functional to cross-functional focus
- Development of upstream and downstream supply chain relationships from 'arm's length' relationships towards more collaborative partnership relations
- Development of supplier management towards supply chain management

The shift to supply chain management

TRADITIONAL WAYS	NEW WAYS
Key feature: Independence	*Key feature: Integration*
Independent of next link	Dependency
Links are protective	End-to-end visibility
Uncertainty	More certainty
Unresponsive to change	Quicker response
High cost, low service	High service, lower cost
Fragmented internally	'Joined up' structures
'Blame' (adversarial) culture	'Gain' (collaborative value-adding) culture
Competing companies	Competing supply chains

Drivers of supply chain evolution:

- Shorter product lifecycles
- Product proliferation and mass customisation
- Reduced product costs
- Competition

- Increased customer demands
- Need to survive in the age of the 'virtual enterprise'

Competition and collaboration

Shortcomings of adversarial relations:

- The emphasis on competition, rather than co-operation, means that each party fails to derive the full benefits of the other party's expertise (let alone potential synergies).
- More waste arises from the breadth and lack of development of the supply base.
- Suppliers are unlikely to be focused or motivated by short-term contracts.
- There is little potential for improved quality and reduced costs arising from integration and co-operation.

The nature of collaborative relationships:

- Relationship management is based on trust, mutual obligation and co-evolution.
- The supplier participates proactively with the buyer in looking for improvements and innovations.
- Information will be shared more or less freely.

Drivers of supply chain collaboration:

- Whole supply chains – not just individual firms – compete with each other in the global marketplace.
- Product lifecycles have shortened.
- Organisations are increasingly outsourcing non-core activities.
- ICT developments have enabled and supported inter-organisational networking and relationships.
- There is pressure for companies to protect and leverage their intellectual property, knowledge, relationship networks and brand values.
- Arms' length, opportunistic transactions fail to leverage the competitive and value-adding potential in supply chain relationships.
- There are costs of adversarial relationships.
- With competitive pressures towards 'lean' supply, closer relationships and integration help to reduce waste in supply chains.
- 'Best practice' supply techniques, such as total quality management and just in time supply, reduce tolerance for delays and errors in the supply process.
- From the supplier's point of view, there has been a shift towards relationship marketing.

The point is not to advocate one type of relationship over another. 'What is needed is a balance between both approaches and a sophisticated understanding of which tactic to use to develop the strategic goals of the organisation.'

Industry-level collaborative strategies may embrace organisations and constituencies including the following.

- Suppliers and distributors
- Competitors

- Customers
- Other stakeholders

PADI frameworks for collaboration

The PADI framework describes values, drivers and priorities – and can thus be applied to locate the position of organisations (and their stakeholders) on a wide range of issues.

The PADI framework

OBJECTIVE FOCUS

EXTERNAL EMPHASIS	**Pragmatism** *Need for order and getting things done* *Key driving forces:* focus, speed, time, action, performance results, outputs, goals, energy	**Administration** *Need for control and order* *Key driving forces:* systems, control, measurement, analysis, accuracy, detail, methodical, regular, incremental adjustment, consistent	INTERNAL EMPHASIS
	Divergence *Need for difference and change* *Key driving forces:* quantum change, innovation, flexibility, individuality, newness, surprise	**Integration** *Need for integration and cohesion* *Key driving forces:* participation, consultation, teamwork, co-operation, consensus, cohesion, group, partnership	

SUBJECTIVE FOCUS

This basic framework can be used in a number of ways to support the development of collaboration. For example, they can be used:

- To understand the values and needs of customers, suppliers and other stakeholders
- To determine the strategic priorities of the organisation and/or its supply chain partners
- To analyse the strategic and cultural compatibility of supply chain partners
- To determine the best supply structures and collaborations for different logistics service propositions.

Creating collaborative relationships

Factors involved in shifting towards long-term partnership relations:

- Monitoring and managing risks of being 'locked into' longer-term ties
- Improving communication at all levels and points of contact between the organisations
- Implementing or improving performance measurement
- Ensuring strategic as well as operational 'fit' between the organisations
- Monitoring 'trade-offs' in the objectives of the alliance

Trust means having confidence in the truthfulness, integrity, competence and reliability of another person or party – and acting accordingly (eg by delegating tasks to them, or proceeding with your own plans on the basis that they will do what they have said they will do).

Six key elements to developing high-trust supplier relationships:

- Model the behaviours you expect.
- Keep and exceed commitments.
- Proactively develop trust.
- Disclose information.
- Measure trust.
- Be empathetic.

Processes in which suppliers can develop collaboration with customers in B2B markets:

- Forecasting and replenishment
- Order management
- Invoice reconciliation and automation
- Inventory management
- Transportation management

Six steps to implementing partnership sourcing:

- Step 1: Which markets and which products and services
- Step 2: Sell the idea
- Step 3: Choose your partners
- Step 4: Define what you want from the partnership relationship
- Step 5: Make your first partnering relationship work
- Step 6: Refine and develop

Shared services

Shared services are those support functions that are used by many different departments or business units within a large organisation (finance, IT, human resources etc). A shared service unit (SSU) is a dedicated provider of such services to internal users. Individual business units effectively 'outsource' their need for specialist services to a shared provider.

Potential benefits from the introduction of a shared services unit:

- Improved experience for external customers
- Faster and more accurate handling of routine administrative or support work
- Access to expertise through a single point of contact
- Access to information on a 'self-service' basis
- Consolidation of end-to-end procurement processes
- Opportunities to identify and obtain economies of scale.

Criticisms of the SSU approach:

- They may encourage a centralised approach that stifles innovation and initiative.
- Their value and performance levels are not easily measured.
- They may sacrifice effectiveness in favour of efficiency in order to achieve predetermined service levels.
- Workers in SSUs may be remote from end users.

A buying consortium is a group of separate organisations that combine together for the purpose of procuring goods or services. Benefits:

- By means of enhanced bargaining power, the consortium can obtain discounts that would not be available to individual members.
- A consortium can establish framework agreements, simplifying purchase administration for members.
- Consortium members can pool expertise, knowledge and contacts.

Costs and disadvantages associated with consortium purchasing:

- There are costs and effort associated with communication and coordination, staff development and policy development.
- There is an issue of transparency between consortium members.
- Consortia may suffer from lengthy negotiation and decision processes.
- Members are not obliged to purchase to the agreed specification.
- Very large consortia may fall foul of laws and regulations designed to prevent dominant market players from abusing their dominant market position.

Data integration

Three levels of collaborative technology:

- Electronic communication tools: synchronous conferencing etc
- Electronic conferencing tools to facilitate the sharing of information in an interactive way
- Collaborative management tools to facilitate and manage group activities

Increasing systems integration is a feature of procurement and supply chain management maturity. Stages in the process:

- Independence: procurement operates within its own guidelines.
- Dependence: procurement dovetails with other functions via consultation and reporting.
- Business integration: procurement systematically integrates with other functions in the internal supply chain.
- Chain integration: procurement has a key role in securing systematic co-operation and information-sharing across the supply chain.

Drivers for supply chain visibility:

- Customer demand (particularly for global products in competitive markets)
- Cost pressures
- The need to align supply chains with corporate strategy and maximise the supply chain's contribution to enterprise performance.

Technologies for supply chain visibility:

- Enterprise resource planning (ERP) systems
- Integrated supply chain management systems
- 'Dashboard' technology enabling supply chain managers to see identified key progress and performance information
- Other tools enabling the tracking of material and product flows in the supply chain (ideally, as real-time information).
- Business intelligence tools

Risks of data integration: as information and knowledge become increasingly systemised and transparent, so they become more vulnerable. A number of risks may arise from knowledge and information systems, including the gathering of information in supplier databases; the sharing of intellectual property and confidential data with suppliers in the course of collaboration; and the management of relationships via a corporate extranet, negotiations and so on.

Information assurance (IA) is the practice of managing risks related to the use, processing, storage, and transmission of information or data, and the systems and processes used for those purposes. Issues in information assurance:

- Corporate governance
- Contingency, business continuity and disaster recovery planning
- Strategic development and management of IT systems to fulfil the current and future needs of the organisation (and supply chain), while minimising risk, through areas such as systems integration, compatibility, flexibility and security.

OWN NOTES

OWN NOTES

CHAPTER 10

Stakeholder Change Management

Stakeholders in strategic SCM

Stakeholders are individuals and groups who have a legitimate interest or 'stake' in an organisation, process, project or decision.

- Internal stakeholders (eg directors, managers and employees)
- External (primary or connected) stakeholders (eg shareholders, financiers, customers, suppliers, distributors)
- External (secondary) stakeholders (eg government and regulatory bodies, pressure groups, interest groups, professional bodies, trade unions, local community)

The widening of an organisation's responsibilities to less directly connected groups is a major trend in modern business, under the umbrella term of **corporate social responsibility** (CSR).

Stakeholder groups can apply pressure to **influence** organisations in different ways and to different degrees. The more influence a stakeholder has, the more likely it is that managers will have to take that stakeholder's needs and wants into account when developing, communicating and implementing strategy. Stakeholder management recognises the need to take stakeholders into account when formulating strategies and plans.

Mendelow's power/interest matrix

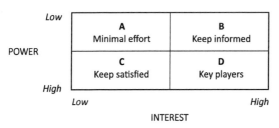

Egan's analysis of stakeholders in a change: partners; allies; fellow travellers; bedfellows; fence sitters; loose cannons; opponents; adversaries; voiceless stakeholders.

Principles of change management

Vision is a cornerstone of strategic change in a corporation – and supply chain. Vision can be **communicated** in various ways, ideally using multiple communication media or vehicles.

Four guiding principles for how to 'get to the vision':

- Business-led: moving from a situation where decisions are made in functional silos to a situation in which decisions are based on total supply chain impact
- Segmented: moving from a situation where decisions are 'one-size-fits-all' to a situation where processes and policies are tailored to relevant customer and supplier segments
- Cost-aware: moving from local initiatives based on limited cost information to a co-ordinated approach to supply chain optimisation, based on shared cost information
- Integrated: moving from transactional, interface-focused models to relational, integration-focused models

Four general factors affecting stakeholder responses to change: facts; beliefs; feelings; values.

Four common sources of resistance to change: parochial self-interest; misunderstanding and lack of trust; contradictory assessments of the situation; low tolerance of change.

Six possible approaches to overcoming resistance to change:

- **Education and communication**, relying on the belief that communication about the need for change, and its benefits, can be used to persuade stakeholders to accept the change programme.
- **Participation and involvement** (or collaboration), based on the belief that stakeholders are more likely to support changes if they are encouraged to own them through having participated in the decision-making process.
- **Facilitation and support**, through which change managers reassure those affected by the change that they will be helped to develop the necessary skills and will be given the necessary resources to achieve the change.
- **Negotiation and agreement**, required where potential resistance groups have considerable power.
- **Manipulation and co-optation**, where resistors are neutralised by co-opting them into the change process.
- **Explicit and implicit coercion,** since change leaders may have the option of simply applying various forms of power, according to the managerial prerogative.

'Planned change represents an intentional attempt to improve, in some important way, the operational effectiveness of the organisation.'

The planned change model (Lewin and Schein)

Eight reasons for failure of transformational change:

- Allowing too much complexity
- Failing to build a coalition of stakeholder support
- Lack of a clear vision for the purpose and direction of change
- Failing to communicate the vision clearly
- Allowing resistance and barriers to gather
- Lack of short-term wins in the change plan
- Stopping short
- Failing to embed changes in the corporate or supply chain culture.

The role of the change agent

Change agents are individuals or teams who are appointed or empowered to drive a change programme: change programme or project managers, external change management consultants, and functional managers pursuing change objectives.

Leaders are individuals (not necessarily in positions of high formal authority) who exercise influence over a group of people or an organisation. Two styles of leadership:

- **Transactional leaders** see the relationship with their followers in terms of exchange.
- **Transformational leaders** see their role as stimulating interest, and inspiring higher achievement and commitment to organisational goals.

Supply chain managers as change agents:

- For internal stakeholders, as the interface between the strategic apex and operating core of the organisation
- For external supply chain stakeholders, as the interface between the organisation and the supply chain
- Through their responsibility for implementation
- Through the provision of advice and feedback to corporate strategists
- Through the driving of 'bottom-up' incremental strategic changes

Advantages of external change agents:

- They are more likely to be objective and dispassionate, without the 'cultural baggage' or personal and factional interests that might bias insiders.
- They may better represent the interests of other stakeholders in the change process and outcomes.
- They are better able to ask questions and perform analyses which challenge the *status quo* and its constraints, and broaden the range of options.
- They may have technical expertise in carrying out research and change interventions which in-house managers lack.
- They are dedicated to the change programme, where internal managers' focus is likely to be dissipated by their workload and other competing priorities.
- They represent a significant, focused investment in change, and may help to signal to stakeholders that the organisation is taking the change process seriously.

Communicating plans

Supply chain strategies can be communicated in various ways, ideally using multiple communication media or vehicles.

- They can be formally incorporated in policy statements, sourcing plans, and other documents.
- Ownership of the strategy must be modelled by management from the top down.

Articulating the strategy in a way that:

- Is compelling, resonant and impactful for stakeholders
- Creates goal congruence, alignment or integration
- Creates incentives, by highlighting potential value gains, benefits or rewards
- Creates momentum and urgency, by highlighting costs, threats or problems
- Minimises potential for misunderstanding and insecurity
- Maximises ownership and identification with strategic values and goals

Aims of effective consultation and engagement processes:

- To allow the views and needs of stakeholders to be taken into account
- To develop change objectives and processes that are likely to be accepted or supported by stakeholders
- To ensure accountability for change decisions which affect stakeholders
- To enhance the quality of change plans through information inputs from expert and involved stakeholders
- To provide for issues management
- To provide for crisis management

Mechanisms and media available for consultation and stakeholder marketing:

- Steering groups, task forces, committees and cross-functional teams
- Setting up temporary advisory or task-force teams for the purpose
- Implementing consultation programmes targeted to key stakeholder groups or stakeholders in particular affected areas
- Issuing proposals and inviting the views and responses of interested parties
- Unveiling proposals at meetings or seminars

Systematic plan for communication with stakeholders to ensure that:

- The correct audience is identified and targeted
- All affected stakeholders are reached with the information
- Information is spread to the right people at the right time in the right way to achieve the most positive effect
- Information is spread efficiently and cost-effectively
- Information can be updated regularly where necessary
- Messages are coherent and consistent
- Confidential information is spread on a 'need to know' basis
- Inaccurate rumours and misinformation are neutralised

- Opportunities are given, where appropriate, to gather feedback and deal with concerns or resistance on the part of stakeholders
- The process is monitored and later reviewed.

Elements in a stakeholder communication plan:

- A list of all stakeholders and their information requirements
- Communication mechanisms to be used
- Key elements of information to be distributed by the different mechanisms
- Roles and responsibilities of key individuals
- Identification of how unexpected information from other parties will be handled within the scope of the activity.

Gauging the acceptance of strategic change

Responses to influencing attempts (such as the roll-out of strategic change initiatives) take three basic forms: resistance, compliance and internalisation (or acceptance).

Resistance means that stakeholders position themselves against the change, and actively attempt to avoid having to comply with it.

Compliance means that stakeholders are willing to do what is requested of them as part of the change programme, but no more. Compliance may be sufficient in some contexts: where the work is highly programmed or automated, for example.

Internalisation or acceptance means that stakeholders are brought to agree internally with the need and/or value of the strategic change: it is aligned with their own goals, beliefs and interests, so that they are able to buy into it in a committed way.

OWN NOTES

CHAPTER 11

Measuring Supply Chain Performance

Performance measurement processes

We measure performance against:

- *Defined performance criteria* (such as KPIs or service level agreements)
- *Previous performance,* to identify deterioration or improvement trends
- *The performance of other organisations* or standard *benchmarks*

Five main reasons for supply chain performance measurement:

- Performance management systems provide an effective framework for management decision-making.
- Performance measures facilitate all-directional and cross-functional, performance-focused communication through the organisation and supply chain.
- Performance measures direct the behaviour of the members of the organisation and supply chain in pursuit of desired goals.
- Effective performance management fosters innovation and improvement.
- Performance measures help organisations and supply chains to evaluate their competitive positioning and capabilities.

Benchmarking is: 'Measuring your performance against that of best-in-class companies, determining how the best-in-class achieve these performance levels and using the information as a basis for your own company's targets, strategies and implementation'.

Four types of benchmarking: internal benchmarking; competitor benchmarking; functional benchmarking; generic benchmarking.

Stages in a benchmarking process: market and supply chain analysis to determine priorities and success factors; identify suitable comparators; research and assess comparator's performance and processes; analyse research feedback to identify best practice and performance gaps; plan new or modified processes, set targets, plan and implement change.

11

Joint performance appraisal systems – objectives:

- To recognise the impact of buyer-side processes and behaviours
- To identify problems within the buyer-supplier relationship

- To support long-term value-adding relationships
- To encourage collaboration on continuous measurable improvements

Key performance indicators

Key performance indicators (KPIs) are clear qualitative or quantitative statements which define adequate or desired performance in key areas (critical success factors), and against which progress and performance can be measured. Where possible, such goals will be *quantitative:* that is, numerical or statistical.

SMART objectives: specific; measurable; attainable; relevant; time-bounded.

Distinguishing characteristics of good performance measures:

- They are directly related to objectives and strategies.
- They are comprehensive and well balanced.
- They are understandable but not underdetermining.
- They are meaningful: providing management with focus and direction for action.
- They vary between locations and customer segments.
- They vary over time, taking account of STEEPLE factors, customer requirements and changing corporate objectives.
- They provide fast feedback.

Setting KPIs for *supplier* or *supply chain* performance, in particular, may be beneficial for strategic supply chain management in the following areas.

- Setting clear performance criteria and expectations
- Managing identified supply chain risks
- Focusing attention on integrated performance measures and critical success factors for the supply chain as a whole, in order to minimise sub-optimal behaviour
- Supporting performance management and improvement
- Identifying high-performing suppliers and relationships
- Providing feedback for learning and continuous improvement in the supply chain and buyer-supplier relationship management.

Process for developing KPIs: identify CSFs; determine measures of success or improvement for each CSF; develop and agree KPIs with key stakeholders.

Performance measurement at different levels

STRATEGIC	TACTICAL	OPERATIONAL
Lead time or agility against norm	Efficiency of order cycle	Delivery performance (OTIF)
Quality status and aspirations	Quality assurance methodology	Quality conformance or non-conformance rates
Future growth, innovation, and/ or integration potential	Capacity flexibility	Technical support levels
Cost saving initiatives and potential	Cashflow management	Speed of response to change in planned requirements
Risk management processes		
Technology leverage		
Supply chain management capability		

The performance pyramid

The performance pyramid illustrates the integration and alignment of performance measures at different, clearly defined levels of the organisation. The strategic apex and the operational core of the organisation are linked by:

- The flow-down and translation of objectives from the top down and
- The implementation of measures from the bottom up.

'Once the customer service objectives have been set at the business operating system level and the key measures developed at the local operational level, all departments involved in the delivery of products or services must be identified. Measures that represent successful hand-offs between the departments can then be developed. These measures force the departments to focus not only on how effectively each department or group operates, but also on improving the performance of the whole system rather than risking sub-optimisation' (Nuthall).

The balanced scorecard

The balanced scorecard is an approach to performance measurement that combines traditional financial measures with non-financial measures, using both quantitative and qualitative metrics. The balanced scorecard approach to performance measurement provides management with a more integrated and balanced framework of metrics that can be cascaded to all levels of the business (and supply chain) and used in pursuit of overall corporate objectives.

Four key perspectives:

- *Financial:* financial performance and the creation of value for shareholders

11

- *Customers:* how effectively the organisation delivers value to the customer, and develops mutually beneficial relationships with customers and other stakeholders
- *Internal business processes:* how effectively and efficiently value-adding processes are carried out throughout the supply chain
- *Innovation and learning:* the skills and knowledge required to develop distinctive competencies for future competitive advantage and growth.

The 'balance' of the scorecard is thus between: financial and non-financial performance measures; short-term and long-term perspectives; and internal and external focus.

Working with a balanced scorecard requires identification and description of several factors for each perspective selected.

- The organisation's long-term goals
- The critical success factors (CSFs) in achieving those goals
- The key activities which must be carried out to achieve those success factors
- The key performance indicators (KPIs) which can be used to monitor progress.

There are drawbacks and limitations to the balanced scorecard approach in practice. Developing and implementing the scorecard is a complex and time-consuming exercise. It will often imply radical change of management style and organisation culture – for which resources and support may not be available. Commitment from senior management must be genuine and consistent to avoid 'mixed messages' (eg if lip service is paid to the balanced scorecard, but procurement is still judged mainly on its ability to reduce costs...)

A structured scorecard cascading approach enables the supply chain function to establish a set of strategically-orientated performance metrics in support of overall corporate objectives. In addition, these developed metrics provide supply chain managers with a comprehensive view of the organisation's objectives and performance that in turn informs supply chain performance measurement. The concept of the scorecard has been extended to supplier enterprises where the associated metrics are commonly referred to as **supplier balanced scorecard (SBS).**

The dashboard concept

Dashboard metrics is a user-friendly tool allowing managers to 'take the pulse' of operations at any given time, by highlighting a few key indicative performance metrics, which can be monitored in real time. The model suggests that 5–7 metrics be selected across four key categories: operational cost, time and response, profitability and margins, and customer service.

Gathering performance feedback

Gathering data for performance measurement:

- *Continuous monitoring* may be possible in some contexts.
- More generally, performance may be monitored at *key stages* of a process, project or contract.

- *Periodic reviews* are often used: examining results against defined measures or targets at regular or fixed intervals.
- *Post-completion reviews* are often used for projects and contracts.

Feedback mechanisms for gathering data on supplier performance, and comparing them against relevant performance measures:

- The gathering of feedback from internal and external customers and other stakeholders, using feedback groups, complaint procedures, project reviews and survey questionnaires
- The gathering of performance information through observation, testing (eg quality inspections), and analysis of documentation, transaction records and management reports (eg analysis of inspection reports, complaint and dispute records and so on)
- Budgetary control: monitoring actual costs against budgeted or forecast costs
- Formal performance reviews or appraisals (sometimes called 'vendor rating' exercises)
- Contract management, continually monitoring compliance with contract terms
- Regular meetings between buyer and supplier representatives
- Project management
- The use of consultants to monitor compliance with quality standards, benchmarks or ethical standards
- The use of technical specialists to monitor supplier performance

Systematic post-contract performance appraisal and evaluation is often referred to as 'vendor rating'. Vendor rating is the measurement of supplier performance using agreed criteria or KPIs, using techniques such as appraisal survey questionnaires, interviews and site visits.

The concept of 360-degree feedback (or multi-source appraisal) was originally pioneered for use in individual performance appraisals. The individual is rated by a range of selected internal and external stakeholders in their performance (eg managers, direct reports and team members, peers, and customers and suppliers), alongside self-appraisal reporting. The same principles of multi-source feedback can be used in joint performance appraisal and supplier performance.

11

OWN NOTES

CHAPTER 12

Developing Supply Chain Capability

Knowledge management

Knowledge management is 'the systematic process that supports the continuous development of individual, group and organisational learning; involving the creation, acquisition, gathering, transforming, transfer and application of knowledge to achieve organisational objectives'.

A systematic approach to knowledge management:

- *Acquiring* knowledge
- *Generating or creating* knowledge
- *Transforming* information into new knowledge
- *Capturing* unspoken, internal (tacit) knowledge to convert it to open, stated (explicit) knowledge, so that it can be communicated, shared and used
- *Organising* knowledge
- *Storing* knowledge effectively in information and knowledge management systems
- *Sharing or disseminating* knowledge throughout the organisation
- *Maintaining* knowledge
- *Protecting* distinctive, value-adding knowledge for competitive advantage
- *Applying* knowledge to develop core capabilities

Seven drivers for systematic knowledge management in organisations:

- Business pressure for innovation
- Inter-organisational enterprises
- Networked organisations, and the need to co-ordinate geographically dispersed groups
- Increasingly complex products and services with a significant knowledge component
- Hyper-competitive global markets
- The digitisation of business environments and the ICT revolution
- Concerns about the loss of organisational knowledge, due to increasing downsizing, outsourcing and staff mobility.

12

The Nonaka-Takeuchi model

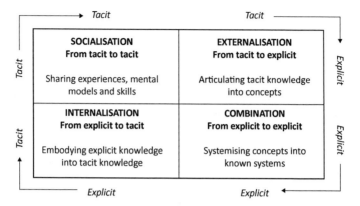

Challenges of knowledge management:

- Getting employees on board
- The role of technology
- Lack of business goals for knowledge management
- Lack of dynamism and flexibility
- Confusion of information and knowledge

Key processes where learning organisations excel: experimentation; learning from past experience; learning from others; transferring knowledge.

Developing procurement and supply chain competencies

Learning and development may occur on four levels.

- Individual: including personal, skill and career development
- Group development
- Occupational and professional development
- Organisational development

Supplier development activities are an important part of knowledge, skill and competence development in the supply chain, in order to:

- Develop strategic, competitive threshold and core competencies in the supply chain
- Develop supplier knowledge of the buying organisation's business needs, markets, processes and aspirations
- Support and facilitate suppliers in meeting specific capability requirements
- Support and facilitate suppliers in improving performance against agreed KPIs and improvement targets

Five-step model to develop supply chain skills: define what supply chain competency means to the organisation; match people with required skills levels; develop the skills-building curriculum; make the delivery commitment; evaluate and improve.

Development needs analysis

Some development requirements may emerge relatively informally in the course of work.

- Changes in legislation, technology or sourcing and supply methods create a knowledge or skill gap.
- Critical incidents may be observed or reported and then analysed.
- Developmental discussions may be used to identify performance 'gaps' and required interventions.
- Career and continuing professional development activities may lead individuals to self-nominate for training or development.

Knowledge and skill needs may also, however, need to be more systematically assessed.

Training needs analysis:

- Measuring what employees need to be *able* to do in order to perform a job competently and in line with performance standards
- Measuring what employees actually *can* do
- Identifying any 'gap' between the two, as a potential need for learning, training and development.

In more detail:

- Define the required level of competence for the job.
- Measure the present level of employees' competence.
- Compare present competence with benchmark or target performance: identify knowledge or skill gaps (gap analysis).
- Design and implement interventions (including training) to remedy those gaps.
- Monitor, review and feed back on progress as appropriate.

SWOT analysis

INTERNAL	**Strengths** New technology Quality management systems Stable, high quality staff Market leading brands	**Weaknesses** Low new product development Poor financial controls Non-renewable resources
EXTERNAL	**Opportunities** E-commerce Consumer values re quality Tax breaks for regional development	**Threats** Environmental protection law Fashion trends Ageing demographic

12

Training and development

Off-the-job training methods:

- Lectures, classes and/or open or distance learning programmes
- The use of case studies, role plays, in-tray exercises and so on
- Visits and tours
- Development centres
- E-learning

On-the-job training methods:

- Orientation or induction training
- Coaching
- Mentoring
- Action learning

Experiential learning:

- Practice, feedback, reflection and adjustment (learning by 'trial and error'), using everyday work as a learning and improvement opportunity
- Temporary promotions or 'assistant to' positions
- Project or committee work

Reasons for increased attention to management development:

- Management development can promote improved performance capability.
- Management development supports management succession.
- Organisational support for career development may help the organisation to attract and retain quality managerial talent.

Management development programmes typically involve some form of formal management education and training.

Evaluating training and development activity – the Kirkpatrick model:

- Level 1: **trainee reactions** to the experience can be measured.
- Level 2: **trainee learning** can be measured, to see how far the programme met specific learning objectives.
- Level 3: **changes in trainees' job behaviour** and performance can be measured, to measure how far learning has been transferred or applied to on-the-job tasks.
- Level 4: **performance** can also be monitored at a higher level to assess the impact of training on organisational results and culture: for example, supply chain performance.

Performance management

Performance management is the process by which shortfalls and weaknesses in individual and team performance are identified and addressed through various types of improvement or development intervention, on an ongoing basis.

Four key activities in performance management:

- Preparation of performance agreements (also known as performance contracts)
- Preparation of performance and development plans
- Management of performance throughout the year
- Performance review and appraisal

Appraisal is: 'the regular and systematic review of performance and the assessment of potential, with the aim of producing action programmes to develop both work and individuals.'

Stages in a typical performance appraisal system:

- Identification (or review) of criteria for assessment
- Preparation of an appraisal report by the appraisee's manager
- An appraisal interview
- Provision for review of (or appeal against) the appraisal
- Preparation, agreement and implementation of action plans
- Follow-up monitoring of progress

Ways in which managers can monitor, measure and review team members' job performance:

- Observation of job performance
- Work sampling
- Results reporting
- Discussion with individuals
- Team feedback and review meetings
- Feedback gathering from key stakeholders

Feedback assessments may be sought from a range of key stakeholders:

- Peer appraisal
- Upward appraisal
- Internal customer appraisal
- Appraisal of buyer performance by suppliers

360-degree feedback (or **multi-source appraisal**) is based on the recognition that the employee's immediate boss is not the only (or necessarily the best) person to assess his performance.

OWN NOTES